Brown Girl MAGIC
Affirmations book

Written By
Heaven Jackson and
Danielle Jackson
Illustrated By
Danielle Jackson

I am brave.

I am beautiful Inside and out.

I am confident.

My skin, hair, brown eyes and my smile are amazing!

I never give up.

I am loved.

I am
Kind and
friendly to
others.

I am loving.

I am strong.

I can do anything I put my mind to.

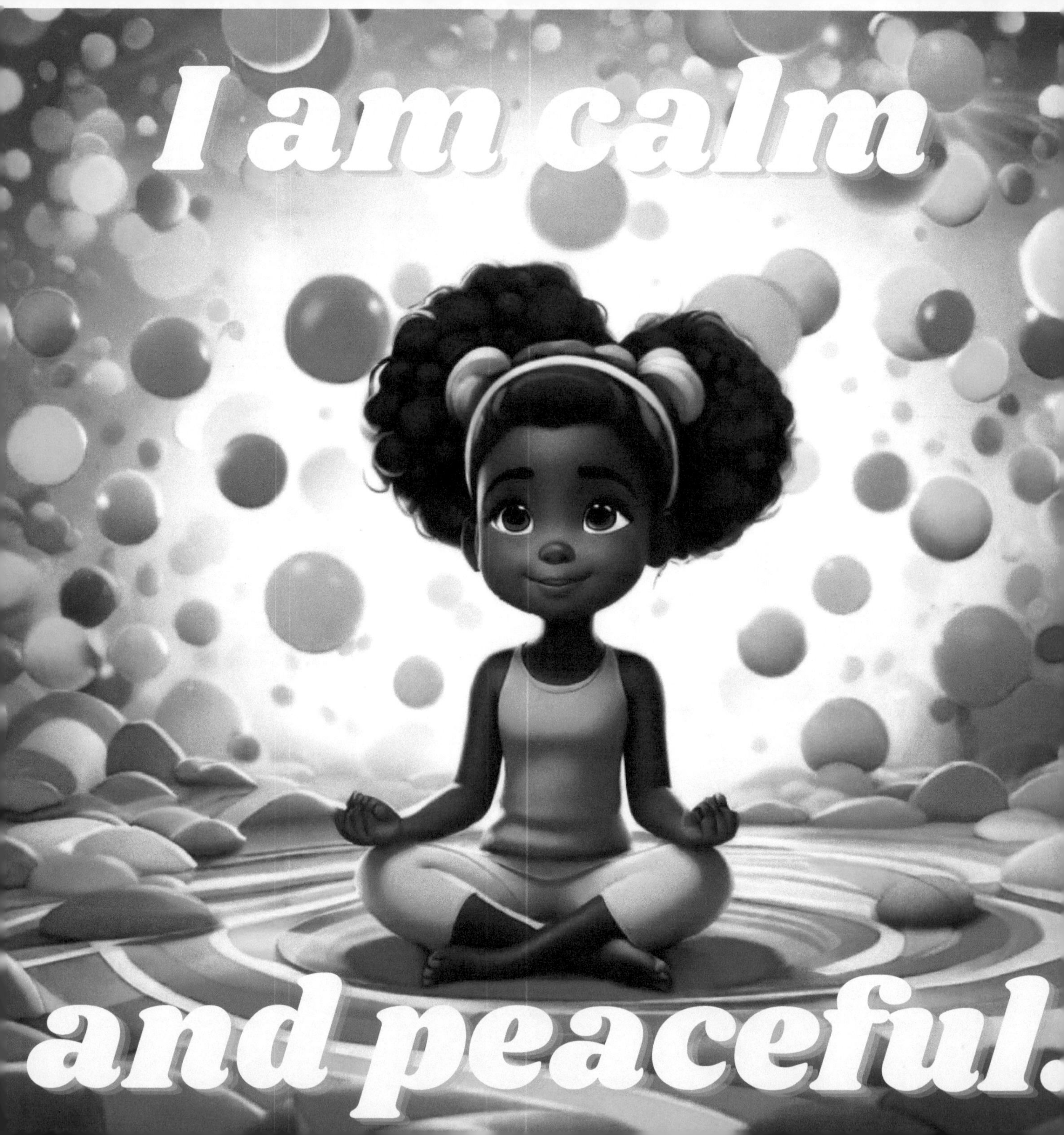

I am calm and peaceful.

I am

happy and
healthy.

I am

connected
to nature.

I am
blessed.

I matter.

I love
myself.

We are more than enough.

Brown Girl Magic is a book that celebrates the beauty, strength, and diversity of brown girls. It is a book that teaches them to love themselves, to be confident, and to know their worth. It is a book that empowers them to follow their dreams, to overcome obstacles, and to make a difference in the world. Brown Girl Magic shows brown girls that they are amazing and magical.

The book is written by Danielle and Heaven Jackson, a mother-daughter duo who want to inspire brown girls through their words and stories.